What Kind of Man Is Joseph, and What Kind of Man Are You?

What Kind of Man Is Joseph, and What Kind of Man Are You?

Eugene Blair

DISCIPLESHIP RESOURCES

PO BOX 340003 • NASHVILLE, TN 37203-0003
www.discipleshipresources.org

Cover design by Bill Tyler

Interior design by PerfecType, Nashville, TN

ISBN 978-0-88177-561-7

Library of Congress Control Number: 2008911695

For information regarding rights and permissions, contact Discipleship Resources, PO Box 340003, Nashville TN 37203-0003; fax 615-340-1789.

Contents

Preface

> **Glean:** *to collect or scrape together in small quantities; to gather after the harvest; to collect bit by bit.*

Using Joseph's story in Matthew as a foundation, the purpose of this book is to guide men (single, married, or in a committed relationship) through any season of the year or time of spiritual journeying. This study is particularly beneficial at Advent/Christmas and is suitable for individual and group study. The focus is personal discipleship and inner growth for men, helping them in their relationships with self, God, family, and others. By studying Joseph, men will come to appreciate his quiet and discerning spirit, commitment, and inner strength. This book focuses on seeing Joseph as a model for fostering and maintaining relationships that are enduring, whole, committed, and supportive of our spouses, friends, and partners.

After the introduction, each chapter follows a pattern for reflection and study that includes the following sections:

1. Narrative—based on the theme;
2. Making It Real Everyday—applying the theme to everyday living;
3. A Reflection Journal—personal reflections on the theme.

The appendix contains a group reflection guide, which provides instruction for a five-week, a one-hour group reflection process.

Mary and Joseph: A Tragic Love Story

> And Jacob begat Joseph the husband of
> Mary, of whom was born Jesus, who is
> called the Christ (Matthew 1:16, *KJV*).

Matthew's opening chapters read like a
romance novel. Set in the New Testament,
there are stories about birth, love, sex, marriage,
pregnant women, and relationships. Matthew's
Christmas story may not be as popular as the
one in the Gospel of Luke, but it is a great love
story about a young Jewish couple caught up in
the ultimate timing of God's action in the
world, that is, the birth of the Savior.
Underneath the centuries-honored testament of
Matthew, there is a traditional Jewish wedding
turned tragic. And yet, I believe there are lessons, simple gleanings for men about how to
grow in their spiritual journeys.

You know the story. Mary was engaged or
betrothed to Joseph. In biblical times, that was

the same as being married. Though they were forbidden to have sexual relations while engaged, others referred to them as husband and wife. Therein lies the problem: before they came together, Mary was found to be with child.

The tradition was that a pledge or betrothal constituted an exchange of vows. This was followed by a one-year period of waiting before the bride entered the husband's house. At that point, they could consummate the marriage. Society dictated that marriage could only be broken by a divorce. The law stated that anyone having relations with a pledged woman could be put to death. This applied to the man and woman (Deut. 22:23-24).

Joseph was faced with a difficult choice upon learning of Mary's pregnancy. Because Mary was found to be with child, her apparent unfaithfulness carried a severe social and religious stigma. According to Jewish law, Joseph could have accused her of fornication and called for an immediate divorce. The divorce laws in those days were very liberal and highly favored the man. The Jewish authorities also had a right to stone her to death. These were tough issues for a Jewish man in Palestine.

Perhaps Joseph thought these were in fact

his only two choices. After all, he knew the law well. But God had a third option—marry her anyway. Matthew's text does not say, but in view of the dire circumstances, this third option surely had not occurred to Joseph. It might not have occurred to any of us in that predicament. Through a dream and an angelic visit, God showed Joseph there was more here than he had thought or imagined. While Joseph seemed to be taking a course of prudent action for both Mary and himself, God guided him to a different decision.

Thanks to the gospels, the Christian tradition has harvested a joyous crop of music, liturgy, and spirituality for Advent and Christmas. Is there anything left to glean from Matthew's Christmas story for men? After all, Joseph stands silently by while Elizabeth and Mary get the primary roles in all the Christmas plays and the baby gets all the attention. I believe there is! I believe men need and want biblical models for their spirituality. Men can learn a great deal from Joseph's situation, and the decisions he made throughout the story can inform them. Joseph showed us some special life qualities that can help us on our own journeys to know God and to live in this world where the roles, expectations, and places of men are often confusing and constantly changing.

What Kind of Man Is This?

I re-discovered Joseph as a pastor searching for resources for our men's group. When our group at church wanted to do a Bible study, they turned to me as the pastor to lead it. I decided to write one for them. I never considered Joseph a spiritual mentor until I studied and re-experienced his story in Matthew 1-2. I saw him with the eyes and ears of a man. It was here that I found a dynamic man of God who was more than a silent partner in a Christmas story. He offered to men disciplines and convictions worth striving for.

What kind of man is Joseph? Let's take a look at the opening chapters of Matthew's Christmas story from Joseph's point of view. Joseph is the earthly key to the incarnation, how Jesus, the Son of God, was born into the world. Joseph's story is full of the unexpected: dreams, danger, late-night escapes, and evil kings. It is full of intimacies between men, women, and their children. Through Joseph, Matthew reveals an important truth about

Jesus' humanity. Jesus, "the Lord saves," came to earth as Savior because we could not do it by ourselves. In part, this took place because Joseph chose to keep faith with God, to be committed.

I believe that the love a man has for a woman led Joseph to act in the way he did toward his betrothed. It was this love that opened Joseph's mind and spirit to receive those heavenly visitors in his dreams and discern the calling of God on his life. It was this same love coupled with a strong sense of commitment that compelled Joseph to bring Mary into his house, to refrain from sexual union with her, and to stand by her as she gave birth to their first-born son.

What Happened to Joseph the Father of Jesus?

The life of Joseph is somewhat of a mystery to us. We know very little about him or the early years of Jesus' life prior to his public ministry. The gospels offer very little regarding any childhood events beyond Christ's birth except one reference found in Luke. It is the very last time the Bible ever mentions Joseph, the adoptive father of Jesus. Luke 2:41-51 reads:

Every year his parents went to Jerusalem for the Feast of the Passover. When he was twelve years old, they went up to the Feast, according to the custom. After the Feast was over, while his parents were returning home, the boy Jesus stayed behind in Jerusalem, but they were unaware of it. Thinking he was in their company, they traveled on for a day. Then they began looking for him among their relatives and friends. When they did not find him, they went back to Jerusalem to look for him. After three days they found him in the temple courts, sitting among the teachers, listening to them and asking them questions. Everyone who heard him was amazed at his understanding and his answers. When his parents saw him, they were astonished. His mother said to him, "Son, why have you treated us like this? Your father and I have been anxiously searching for you." "Why were you searching for me?" he asked. "Didn't you know I had to be in my Father's house?" But they did not understand what he was saying to them. Then he went down to Nazareth with them and was obedient to them. But his mother treasured all these things in her heart. And Jesus grew in wisdom and stature, and in favor with God and men (*NIV*).

We can only suppose that Joseph died during the quiet years of Jesus' early life, before he became a public figure. We do know that he trained Jesus in the trade of carpentry. We do know that Joseph and Mary had children after Jesus was born: James, Joses, Simon, and others. Perhaps, for our purposes, the cause or timing of Joseph's death is not nearly as important as the strength of character he displayed. In first hearing about Mary's pregnancy, Joseph did not want to subject Mary to public scorn. After hearing from an angel who confirmed Mary's incredible and mysterious story, Joseph obediently accepted the role of the adopting father of the baby Jesus, the Christ child.

So, all we have is the last reference about Joseph in Luke. Luke confirms that Joseph was a devout follower of the customs of his religion with his observance of Passover. The passage implies that Joseph led the way and made certain there was good spiritual training for the children in his family. Joseph proved his integrity and willingness to be obedient to God's direction and guidance.

Let's Begin

Come and let's glean together the bits and pieces that make up this man called Joseph. Begin by reading the entirety of Matthew 1 and 2 in one sitting. Get into the story, the characters, the dreams, the turn of events, and the themes. Start your reading with this prayer:

> Loving God, as I read and study about your servant Joseph, visit me as you visited him in such glorious and mysterious ways. Make yourself known to me so that I, too, may rise up and follow wherever you lead me. Guide me by your Spirit to make time for reading, reflecting, and praying during this study. Let this season of study be to me a new season of preparation to receive you into my heart and my life. May my ears be attentive to your calling and my heart and mind be open to what you have to teach me in this study. Amen.

CHAPTER ONE

Commitment

> Now the birth of Jesus the Messiah took place in this way. When his mother Mary had been engaged to Joseph, but before they lived together, she was found to be with child from the Holy Spirit.
>
> Matthew 1:18 (*NRSV*)

Commit: to bind; to obligate; to be devoted to a cause or course of action

Narrative

As Matthew unfolds this drama, we notice that Joseph does not utter a single word of dialogue. He says nothing at all. Unlike Job of the Old Testament, he does not complain, criticize, or rebuke God for his situation. Joseph does not gather his friends for a round of mutual discontent and God bashing. Instead, he allowed God to use him to make something possible out of the impossible. Joseph appears to turn the anxiety, worry, and angst of his marriage into new meanings for us today.

To say Joseph was committed is an understatement. For him, there was no turning back or changing his mind. The very thought of such a thing strikes fear in the hearts of many today. What are you committed to in your life? We can easily answer that by looking at our checking accounts and our daily calendars. Sit down and calculate how much time you devote solely to your family and to them alone. How much of your time, talents, and resources do you offer to the ministry of your church? Do you have time for prayer and devotions? Your answers tell the real stories of where your true commitments lie.

This hit home for me one evening after a family supper. I was leaving home for a meeting to help some church members with their vision and mission statement. Now, to put this in perspective, you have to know that it is difficult for my children to understand what I do since I am not a local church pastor. The whole "conference staff person" thing is hard to explain. So I simply tell them I help people know more about Jesus. On this particular night, my then six-year-old daughter asked me where I was going. I said, "I am going to go help people know about Jesus." She, being tired of my many evening meetings, replied, "I wish you would stay home and tell me about Jesus." She convicted me for my commitments and for an unbalanced personal calendar. I needed to make some changes.

Matthew does not tell us that Joseph was committed to God, Mary, and his son. Matthew tells nothing of his relationship to the other children in his family. We can only learn this from his actions. This all started because he was committed to obeying the law and went to be enrolled in the Roman census (Luke 2:1-3). Through the ordeals of the opening chapters of Matthew, though he had choices, Joseph was committed to the course God set out for his life. After all, none of his family or friends would have blamed him if he had dumped Mary at the steps of the first synagogue he could find. She was pregnant, and he was not the father. Jewish religion supported him, and the law was in his favor. But, being a righteous and just man, Joseph stood by his commitment.

My family lives in the large metropolitan community of Detroit. The number of young single women having and raising children is staggering. I often wonder about the young fathers. What roles do they have with the young mothers of their children? What has happened to their lives? How do we in the community support these young families and help these children grow into adulthood? I often wonder if anyone taught these young men about commitment and doing the right thing. As a mentor of young boys, I see my primary role as teaching them about commitment, about respect for women, and about how to care for themselves so that they can grow into mature adulthood. This is my commitment to these young men, the mothers of their children, and their children.

To be committed means to see things through to the end and not to give up when the going gets rough. To be committed to anything in life means to be willing to be unhappy for a while knowing commitment and patience will be blessed by God. This seems to be most difficult in our relationships with others. Consider modern-day marriage. I once heard it said that marriage is a never-ending commitment to an ever-changing and unknowable person. It takes more than just love; it takes commitment.

So, Joseph made a difficult choice for a young man just engaged to a woman who was pregnant. Certainly he knew that taking Mary as his wife was going to be a troubling and humiliating experience. Yet, he was committed. He chose to obey God and follow the angel's command to do the right thing.

Think about your life and the commitments you have made. What kind of man is this, and what kind of man are you, who can make these kinds of choices and decisions? If we want our relationships to be fulfilling, then our wives, families, partners, lovers, and friends need us to be there, fully and totally. They will not respond in kind unless they are assured of our commitment. In order for us to enjoy our relationships and feel fulfilled and whole in them, we must make these kinds of commitments. This is the kind of man Joseph was.

The fear of commitment is epidemic in our culture today. So much of our lives is out of our control. We live in a culture of rapid and unceasing change. We seem unable to keep up with technology, our jobs, and our own personal schedules. The issue for us in all of this is how to keep our primary relationships whole, sustainable, and intimate in the midst of chaos?

Commitment in these times is hard. We can all agree it is not easy.

Why is commitment such a difficult issue in our lives? Perhaps we are responding to the climate around us. No one wants to be tied down. No one wants to sign on for the long haul. We are constantly looking for the next job, the next sexual encounter, the next relationship, or the next career move. We keep our resumés updated and in supply because we never know when a new opportunity will knock. Professional sports teams know that their star players are only a contract away from a new deal with more pay with a new team. Churches and volunteer agencies report that it is harder than ever to get people to give of their time. We would rather lease than buy, shorter is better, and we never fully unpack because the next move is just around the corner.

It is no secret that in modern cultures like ours, single people are in search of the perfect partner, the ultimate mate, the romantic marriage. There is a whole industry devoted to helping them find this perfection. Yet, about half of our marriages end in divorce. Brides and grooms no longer commit to "till death do us part." They commit to "as long as we love each other." It seems when it comes to women, marriage, and relationships, men are accused of being the poster children for fear of commitment. While some if this accusation is justified, much of the situation is simply our culture.

Why does this epidemic of fear of commitment exist? Let's explore three of the possible reasons. First, perhaps we find it hard to break out of the expectation that we should be selfish. Take care of number one first! We are told and taught not to let anything or anyone impede our personal agendas. We prize our personal freedom. Perhaps because so much of life is out of our control, we do not want to be held down or held back by forces within our control, especially other people. To be committed, whether to another person, a job, or an organization, is to let go of some control. Experts say that this is the reason so many people choose to live together rather than marry. After all, in our culture, you never know when the other person's commitment will fail or when you will find greener grass somewhere else.

Secondly, perhaps we are told and taught never to be satisfied with what we have. We always want more. We want more clothes, money, sex, a bigger house, or a newer automobile. We want better relationships, and we want them right now. We want the newest and latest technology. I recently purchased a new cell phone with all of the new personal data electronics. It includes a calendar, address book, video games, calculator, and other gizmos. You can imagine how dismayed I was to go to a meeting and have someone show me the updated version of the one I had just purchased!

We want our houses filled with the latest toys and gadgets to tell us, "We have arrived." The absurdity of this behavior hits home on that bumper sticker that reads, "the one who dies with the most toys wins." Storage facilities with lockers and bins are a growing industry trying to keep up with our need to keep our goods stored, saved, and protected.

Finally, and maybe most importantly, perhaps we are told and taught that individuality is more important than community. We refuse to freely give of ourselves for the good of others. The New Testament teaches us that the Christian life is about community and about the behaviors necessary for individuals to live as a community. Community calls for commitment, but we want relationships without costs to us. We want to do our own thing, go our own way, and live our own lives without having to consider and include the well-being of another. Prenuptial agreements and marriage contracts are the magic potion of the modern marriage and relationship. We view them as the silver bullet for those who want life to cost them nothing.

I have chosen to speak about commitment as the first gleaning from Matthew 1-2 because it is foundational to the others. Without commitment to God, ourselves, and our own journey, we cannot expect to grow in love and grace. Without commitment to a spiritual discipline, there will be no satisfaction and joy on the journey.

Maybe it is just as important to talk about confession along with commitment. We must be able to name our issues around commitment before God's healing can take hold. We must confess our selfish drives, our dissatisfaction with what is, and our lack of community. Maybe then the road to commitment will be lit, and we can see the way.

Making It Real Every Day

We all have commitments. We make them, keep them, or break them for various reasons. It would be good to stop every now and then to examine our commitments. Often we feel overworked or overextended or exhausted because we have too many demands and commitments on our plates. We do this because we try to keep ourselves and everyone else happy and pleased with us. In order for us to enjoy the fruits of a committed and sustainable relationship with others, we must be clear about our commitments. By reading this book, you have indicated your concern for your personal life and relationships. What can you do to be clear about the way you make and keep your commitments? Here are some ideas that you can start with today:

- Establish daily prayer and reflection times, and try journaling;
- Join a group for bible study, accountability, and support;
- Be clear about your priorities and how you will use your time;
- Guard your time (this may be the only time in your life when you can be truly selfish!);
- Learn to say no—you cannot do everything and please everyone;
- Take time for self-refreshment, retreat, and reflection;

- Seek out a spiritual friend and guide.

We all must find ways to give time daily to our spiritual journeys. I find that something as simple as a lawn chair in my trunk is helpful. I carry one of those popular lawn chairs collapsed in a bag in my trunk. Because I am on the program staff of our geographically large conference, I travel a great deal, sometimes driving over a thousand miles a month for this ministry. Whenever I get some free time between appointments or traveling, I pull into a park. I get out the lawn chair and sit quietly for a period of time to regroup, reflect, and pray. Surrounding myself with nature and sunshine creates a natural prayer space for me.

Take out a blank piece of paper and draw a line down the middle. On the left side, write down all of the commitments you have today that take up your time. Include job, family, friends, golf, church work, and other activities that take up your day. On the right side, prioritize your commitments. Write a number that indicates which commitment is first, second, third, etc. In other words, number the commitments in terms of how you really want to live your life. Take time to pray, asking God to show you the way to clearer commitments and better use of your God-given time. Close this exercise with this prayer:

> Loving God, in your love you gave me this season of prayer and reflection. You gave me this opportunity to grow in love and grace and commitment. Let me no longer be tossed and thrown around like a ship upon the waves of an angry sea. Come to me daily and help me to anchor my life in you. Lead me in your Spirit as I say *yes* or *no* to the demands on my life. Show me how to seek your kingdom first. Cover me with your grace as I seek to know and to do your will for my life. Amen.

REFLECTION JOURNAL

Find a quiet place where you will be undisturbed for this experience. Light a small candle to remind you of God's presence with you.

Read Matthew 1:18-25

Reflect by putting yourself in Joseph's shoes. Try to imagine what was going through his mind after the visit of the angel. Answer these questions in your journal:

- What is the most difficult aspect of this situation?
- What emotions and feelings are running through this passage?
- Is there a clear call on your life in relationship to this passage?

Rest in the Word

Sit quietly and feast on the Word and your reflections. You may also want to record in your journal new insights, revelations, joys, or concerns that have come out of this experience. Think of ways you may share this experience with those around you.

Prayer

Gracious and loving God, you were in the beginning when the world was created. I come to you in gratitude, aware that your Son came into the world to save the world. You became flesh and lived among us for my sake. Hear me now as I pray for your guidance and encouragement to obey your word, to follow my Brother Jesus, and to walk this daily journey. This I pray In Jesus' name, Amen.

CHAPTER TWO

Awareness

But while he thought on these things, behold, the angel of the Lord appeared unto him in a dream, saying, Joseph, thou son of David, fear not to take unto thee Mary thy wife: for that which is conceived in her is of the Holy Ghost. Then Joseph being raised from sleep did as the angel of the Lord had bidden him, and took unto him his wife: And knew her not till she had brought forth her first-born son: and he called his name JESUS.
Matthew 1:20, 24-25 (*KJV*)

Awareness*: having knowledge or recognition of others; one's own needs, feelings, traits and behaviors; rapport with others*

Narrative

My children and I love going to a bookstore together. They head for the kids' section, and I head for the religion and music sections. I usually have to drag them out to go home. Today, if you go into a bookstore, you will find an abundance of material in the self-help section. Much of it has to do with helping us deal with a wide range of personal issues and how to overcome them. As I have read and reviewed these books over the past twenty-five years of ministry, these self-help gurus and authors have made a dramatic shift. Their books used to tell you how to connect to God and how to have a vital relationship with God in order to have a better personal life. Now, books of this nature are relegated to the religion or spiritual section, which can be small in most stores. The self-help section is now quite large, and the books tell you how to do it all by yourself.

This is an obvious cultural shift. However, a somewhat general idiom in these self-help books is the same: in order to be healed of what ails the mind, body, and spirit, one must become aware. The saying goes, "awareness is healing." That is, healing comes when we are aware of the past and enter the present. It means to understand the behaviors, circumstances, and situations that have caused us heartache, pain, and anguish. In order to grow and change, we must become aware. I want to suggest that we can glean from Joseph's experience a new phrase. That is, "awareness is sensitivity."

A number of years ago, I was the outreach worker on a team for a large children's home. I will never forget the first time I went on a staff retreat with this team led by our director, an experienced social worker. I was new at this idea of retreats. I was struck by the fact that our leader started the retreat by saying, "Let's stop and become aware of our surroundings." Then he began to name all of the things in our surroundings, from the vehicles we arrived in, the roads we traveled to our destination, down to the chairs, the windows, the wall hangings, the coffee pot, etc. It was then that I understood the need to habitually "be aware" of my surroundings; the level of my awareness of people, feelings, and events that are taking place in my sphere of influence reveals how sensitive I really am.

I want to make the case that Joseph, being aware of God's presence in his life and in Mary's, was sensitive to both their needs. His awareness of God's hand on his life opened him up to what God wanted to do with this child to be born, Jesus Christ. Joseph's dreams attest to his awareness and sensitivity to God. There are five dreams in Matthew 1-2, counting the visit of the angel to the Wise Men. Joseph did not wake from his sleep and forget the dreams. He awoke from his dreams and put his life into action for God and his family.

Perhaps you have not thought of a deeper need for awareness as a spiritual practice. Maybe you have not viewed sensitivity as a spiritual discipline or value. This is something we can glean from Joseph's experience.

To be aware and sensitive is more than the notion of "touchy-feely" that many men seem to dislike. It simply means to be aware of the abundance of good and the presence of God in your life and your relationships with others. When you are aware, you are able to take responsibility for your own feelings and needs in order to take into consideration the feelings and needs of others close to you, namely your partner or spouse and children. You begin to see others as children of God and not people who make demands on you. Sensitivity becomes a movement of the spirit upon our hearts that causes us to ask, "What does this child of God need that I can offer?"

I had a life-changing experience many years ago that relates to the practice of awareness. This experience is particularly poignant for me as I write today. One of the youth of our church asked me to go to court with him. He had been arrested and charged with a crime that was going to cost him some serious jail time. His court date was very early on a Monday morning after a busy Sunday of services and church activities that had lasted into the evening. I did not relish the idea of getting up first thing on a cold Monday morning to get to the courthouse for the first round of court appearances. I went with a great deal of anger.

I stood in the outer waiting room with just one other person, a woman who was there for a court date with her son. The guards brought her son down from the lock-up first. His court appearance was short and to the point. When they emerged from the courtroom, they both were in tears and trying to hug each other while the guards tried to pull them apart. Whatever took place in that courtroom was devastating for both of them. The guards pulled them apart and took her son back to lock-up without a word. She stood there looking lost and devastated.

At that time the Spirit of God spoke to me and clearly gave me a message. Did I actually hear a voice? Did God step down from heaven and make God's wishes known to me? I do not know. However, I do know that the Spirit said, "Say something to this woman about the grace and love of God at this point in her life." The Spirit was urging me, as a man of God, to say something to this woman in this moment of her need, to comfort her with words of hope and expressions of kindness. But I was caught up in my needs and anger at my young man for having gotten into trouble and dragging me down there in the first place. So, I said nothing. This woman walked out of the waiting room, down the hall, and out the door back into her world. And the man of God said nothing. I was unaware of my surroundings and those in it. I was insensitive. The scene still haunts me. Lack of awareness leads to deep insensitivity to those around us and results in missed opportunities for spiritual growth.

I wonder if spiritual awareness and sensitivity drew Mary toward Joseph in the first place. After all, it is no secret that women seem to fare better in this arena of human relationships than men. Mary may have seen in Joseph more than an arranged Jewish marriage, as theirs certainly would have been. Perhaps she saw in him the physical strength of a carpenter and adored the roughness of his hard-working hands yet gentle, loving arms to hold her. Maybe she saw in him a kindness she hoped he would pass on to her children. Perhaps she liked the way he treated her so differently from other men in arranged marriages who held all the cards over their wives. Surely, she was aware that she would have dignity, honor, and respect from this man.

All of this, of course, is speculation because Matthew does not tell us, and Joseph speaks not a word. However, we can reasonably glean from his actions that Joseph was a good Jewish man who followed the commandments and ordinances of God. He shows great personal courage when he faces down the conventional wisdom of the day, which was to abandon Mary and end the engagement.

Further, Matthew does not tell us what Mary and Joseph talked about on their long journey from home to Bethlehem. It may have been about the child growing in her womb. As they bumped along the dusty roads, tired and hungry, there must have been some comfort for Mary knowing that the man in her life had an awareness of the presence of God and that he was sensitive to their unexpected predicament and pregnancy.

Joseph was not about to be a stumbling block to the will of God as proclaimed for centuries by the prophets. He could have cried, "Foul, foul!" He could have removed himself from the whole mess. He could have vindicated his hurt and wounded ego by having her stoned to death for apparent adultery. Because of his awareness of the presence of God, he was greatly sensitive and compassionate. God was doing a great thing through Joseph and Mary.

Joseph was a tender, compassionate man who believed that love must temper justice. He had to obey the law of God because the law was clear. How could he obey God in relation to Mary's circumstances? How could he avoid embarrassing her and putting her to shame? After listening to God, it was revealed to Joseph that Mary was not guilty of adultery at all, but was highly favored by God. Joseph asked not only what God's law required, but also how to apply that law in love. Not even Joseph's hurt feelings or his religion's legal requirements could overrule his compassion for Mary. Even in the face of the terrible thing he thought Mary had done to him and to their hopes and dreams, Joseph still had deep feelings for Mary, the person. He could not find it in his heart to harm her in any way. Joseph's awareness and sensitivity are qualities of the Spirit that saved their relationship and, later in Matthew, their very lives.

Making It Real Every Day

I heard someone say in a sermon once that men are like waffles, and women are like spaghetti. By waffles, I do not mean men cannot make up their minds or that they are finicky. I mean men tend to look at life one small piece at a time. Just like squares on a waffle, men tend to take care of one thing at a time, one decision at a time, one task at a time. Surely, this is a generalization, but it is one that I can argue with some degree of certainty. This is certainly the case with my wife and me. She calls her ability to do more than one thing at a time "multi-tasking." I call it confusing!

Women, on the other hand, are like spaghetti. In my experience, I admit with some belligerence that they do tend to be able to multi-task, multi-manage, and multi-attend. Some call this "women's intuition" while some men call it chaos. Again, I can argue this generalization with some degree of certainty.

Herein lies the rub: While trying to relate to each other, men and women often miss each other because they are looking at the same thing through very different lenses. The challenge for men is to be aware and sensitive of themselves, how they live daily, and how all of this affects those around them. Mix waffles and spaghetti together and see what happens. Take any life experience, and you have the makings for confusion: marriage, sex, raising children, spending money, jobs and vocations, doing the dishes, or changing diapers. Men tend to want it done one thing at a time, and women do not understand why men do not like multiple dramas going on all at once.

The call is for men to be aware and sensitive of the God-given differences that make them men. The call on our lives is to love those dear to us in such a way as to make waffles and spaghetti a tasty treat. Often, this means habitually asking a simple question: "How will what I do or say affect my partner?"

REFLECTION JOURNAL

Find a quiet place where you will not be disturbed for this experience. Light a candle to remind you of God's presence.

Read Luke 1:26-38

Consider Mary for a moment:

- How great is her joy at being chosen the handmaiden of God?
- In what ways can you identify with the joy of Mary and confusion of Joseph?
- Where in your life is there a holy joy?
- Who are the people who bring joy into your life?

Rest in the Word

Sit quietly and feast on the Word and your reflections. You may also want to record in your journal new insights, revelations, joys, or concerns that have come out of this experience. Think of ways you may share this experience with those around you.

Prayer

Loving God, I need you in my life. Bring to me again the great joy and possibilities for my life and my relationships. Come to me again, great God of heaven. Heighten my awareness of your presence and strengthen my resolve to walk more closely with you and with those around me. Help men everywhere to be aware of their own needs and concerns, and yet also be available to friends, partners, wives, and children in new and meaningful ways. I ask this in the name of Jesus. Amen.

CHAPTER THREE

Discipline

> And Joseph also went up from Galilee,
> out of the city of Nazareth, into Judaea,
> unto the city of David, which is called
> Bethlehem (because he was of the
> house and lineage of David): To be
> taxed with Mary his espoused wife,
> being great with child.
>
> Luke 2:4-5 (*KJV*)

Discipline: *a system of practices or exercises aimed at training the consciousness for a state of higher and greater spiritual insight, growth, and serenity*

Narrative

Joseph lived and labored under two competing sets of laws, rules, regulations, and expectations. First, he was Jewish. With that came a historical set of religious and spiritual principles he was obligated to obey and follow. Yet, his life was compounded by the presence of the Roman occupation of the Holy Land. With that came another set of rules and obligations laid upon him by the authorities of that day.

We can glean from the Gospel of Luke that Joseph was a man of discipline as he sought to keep faith with both pressures. Both Matthew and Luke tell us virtually nothing about Joseph's prayer life, daily discipline, or religious rigors. However, we can glean from Joseph's actions several conclusions. He followed the law. He responded to the Roman requirement for a census by taking a long and difficult journey with a pregnant woman on a beast of burden. He was a well-read Jewish man who understood the Jewish laws about adultery, marriage, and stoning. We can reasonably speculate that Joseph studied and read the Torah. His daily life included prayer, almsgiving, keeping the commandments, and staying clear of the Roman authorities by doing what they asked.

Men today face similar pressures. The call to work and earn a living takes most of the best of our time. Ever-present family pressures call for personal strength and attentiveness. Circumstances out of our control buffet our vocational goals. Our mental health, moral fortitude, and personal stability are constant sources of anxiety and worry. For example, I live in Michigan, where thousands of jobs have been eliminated or sent overseas. People are leaving the state in droves, bankruptcies are high, and mortgage foreclosures are on the rise. In the midst of all of this, how do we respond to the call to live lives of personal and spiritual holiness and discipline?

Central to the Christian walk is discipline. It is the centerpiece of any spirituality. The term has been used and misused in various ways. The idea of discipline is certainly not as welcome to some as to others. We have all had our negative experiences with discipline. For some of us, the discipline we received as children from adults bordered on abuse when the adults administered it in anger. Perhaps we have failed in some of the personal disciplines we have tried over the years. From getting in shape to finishing a home improvement project, we all have some negative experiences with discipline.

For the Christian who is on a spiritual quest, discipline is the biblical means by which we give over our freedom to a loving God. Discipline is training or practice that leads to a specific spiritual end or produces obedience, self-control, or a specific skill. In spirituality, the goal is a life transformed by the Spirit into the image of Jesus Christ. Discipline is a rule of life or a pattern of living that leads to spiritual growth and Christian community. The church speaks of classical or historical spiritual disciplines such as prayer, Christian conference, fasting, and meditation. There are varieties of expressions of discipline. I heard someone say that for the Christian, discipline is the art of remembering what you really want.

The gospel is a treatise on discipline that grows out of the experience of a believer's active faith in God. Discipline is a moral, ethical, and spiritual call to respond to life on God's terms and not one's own. Jesus' teaching of the Sermon on the Mount in Matthew 5 is an example of this call to a changed life. Discipline allows us to choose between blessing and curse, life and death, change or stagnation.

Perhaps most importantly, discipline gives the believer and the community a deep-seated energy as we respond to the human conditions and circumstances we face. For example, someone said to me on a retreat, "Temptation is the opportunity to see how mature your discipline is." Our call is to respond to life fully influenced by the gospel and the Holy Spirit. Someone else likened spiritual discipline to playing a musical instrument.

Once you have taken the basic lessons, not only can you play, but you can grow and learn more.

What can men do daily to grow in discipline and the Spirit? As a pastor, I have a conflict regarding my spiritual growth. Even though I prepare for work and ministry by writing sermons, preparing Bible studies, drafting worship services, or preparing to lead devotions for others, none of that is really for my growth and journey. It is important for me to distinguish the two by using two different Bibles. I use one Bible for work and another for personal spiritual formation. I know what I am doing for whom by the Bible I choose. This may sound simple, but for me it has been profound. I cannot say that because I am a minister and I do the work of using the Bible daily that I am attending to my faith. I too must be intentional about my personal disciplines and ask, "How is it with my soul?"

Making It Real Every Day

Spiritual leaders have grouped spiritual disciplines in a variety of ways. Let's look at the work of some that are well-known:

Classic Spiritual Disciplines—handed down through the ages of history:

- obedience
- simplicity
- humility
- frugality
- generosity
- truthfulness
- purity
- agape love

The Workbook on Spiritual Disciplines by Maxie Dunam:

- solitude
- prayer
- confession
- study of scripture for guidance
- submission and service
- generosity

The Celebration of Discipline by Richard Foster

- inward disciplines—prayer, meditation, fasting, study
- outward disciplines—simplicity, solitude, submission, service
- corporate disciplines—confession, worship, guidance, celebration

Reaching Out: Three Movements of the Spiritual Life by Henri Nouwen:

- hospitality—reaching out to self

- hospitality—reaching out to others
- hospitality—reaching out to God

Spiritual Disciplines by James Earl Massey:

- prayer
- fasting
- dialogue
- worship

We can see that there is no one single list everyone agrees on, but there is some general agreement. What everyone does seem to agree on is:

- prayer and confession
- solitude
- fasting
- submission and service
- simplicity
- scripture and study

REFLECTION JOURNAL

Find a quiet place where you will not be disturbed for this experience. Light a candle to remind you of God's presence with you.

Read Romans 12:9-21

Paul gives twenty-one commandments or exhortations in this short passage on how to behave like a Christian. Try to imagine what it would take on your part in order for these commandments to take deep root in your life.

- What is the most difficult of these commandments for you right now?
- Look over the many lists of spiritual disciplines. In order for you to behave more like a Christian, are there one or two disciplines that you need to incorporate into your life? Write them down.
- What would it take in order for you to begin a new course of action that includes these one or two spiritual disciplines?
- What are your next steps, beginning today? Write them down and commit yourself to starting today.

Rest in the Word

Sit quietly and feast on the Word and your reflections. You may want to record any new insights, reflection, joys, or concerns that have come out of this experience. Think of ways to share your reflections with those around you.

Prayer

Loving God, I need your gifts in my life today. As you came to Mary and Joseph, come to me in new ways. Give me the gift of a new spirit of spiritual discipline that will lead me to follow you and do your will. I need the gift of a practice and discipline that will open to me the goodness of life around me. I need the gift of a new spirit of grace and openness that will lead me to life eternal. Amen.

CHAPTER FOUR

Righteousness

> The Lord tests the righteous and the wicked, and his soul hates the lover of violence .... For the Lord is righteous, he loves righteous deeds; the upright shall behold his face.
>
> Psalm 11:5, 7 (*NRSV*)

> **Righteousness**: *morally upright; to live without guilt; sin, or shame, to live a life of virtue and morality; to use good judgment and integrity when relating to others*

Narrative

The image should be clear in our minds by now. Joseph and Mary are two teenagers betrothed, which was as good as married in those days and in that part of the world. Mary reports she is pregnant by the Holy Spirit. Picture the turbulence, stress, and chaos in their lives. See Joseph's humiliation and powerlessness. See

Mary's confusion and fear, knowing she was about to be dumped or, worse, stoned to death. They both knew the law and rituals of the Jewish people. See the questions in their minds about this situation now out of their control. The gospel of Luke reports Mary's joy over being chosen the handmaiden of God to give birth to the Savior. But in Matthew, we hear no such good news of great joy.

In the midst of this, we see how Joseph chose to stand firm on the ground of personal and holy righteousness. No matter what translation we use, Matthew 1:19 gives us a picture of Joseph as a righteous man trying to do the right thing:

> Then Joseph her husband, being a just man, and not wanting to make her a public example, was minded to put her away secretly (*NKJV*).

> Because Joseph her husband was a righteous man and did not want to expose her to public disgrace, he had in mind to divorce her quietly (*NIV*).

> And her husband Joseph, being a just man and unwilling to put her to shame, resolved to divorce her quietly (*RSV*).

Righteousness is a character trait of God. Therefore, it is potentially a character trait of the human spirit. To be righteous means to behave and perform in a holy way in one's relationships. It means choosing not to conform to the expectations of the world, family, or friends when faced with difficult moral choices. It means always to strive to take the higher ground while everyone around you clamors for the letter of the law. Because he walked with spiritual integrity, Joseph chose the godly actions of mercy and decency.

Righteousness and Unrighteousness

Righteousness is a spiritual quality one exhibits before God and practices before people. It means to be "just" and to live according to God's standards for relating to people. In the Bible, people who were righteous were different from others. The righteous were set apart and walked with God. To be called righteous was an honor bestowed upon only a few. Those who exhibited righteousness prospered, and those who did not suffered greatly. There is no clearer picture of this for men than when we compare King David with Joseph of Matthew's gospel.

Making It Real Every Day

> Nathan said to David, "You are that man!" (2 Samuel 12:7, *NRSV*).

The story of David and Bathsheba is told in 2 Samuel 11-12. It is the story of a man and a woman, one of the most notorious stories of power, adultery, and murder in the Bible. King David, out for some fresh air on his rooftop, spies the beautiful Bathsheba on another roof. He allows his vision of her to turn to lust and his lust to turn into great sin. When he abuses his power as king and sends for her, he commits adultery and impregnates her. To hide this sin, he sends her husband, Uriah, into a deadly battle where he dies.

The prophet Nathan then confronts King David. Nathan tells David a parable of a greedy, sinful, and power-hungry rich man. When King David cries out in outrage, Nathan confronts him with the words, "You are that man."

The comparison between the events of Joseph's life and David's are obvious. The two men responded to the circumstances of their lives in dramatic ways. To live our lives without morality and decency is unrighteousness. In David's case, unrighteousness meant using his power for his personal gain and needs. It meant abusing a powerless woman and killing a dedicated family man under his command. King David was a great man in many ways. The Bible attests to that. Yet, he allowed the sin of his unrighteousness to get the upper hand in his relationships.

What a contrast to what we know about Joseph! For Joseph, righteousness meant honor, commitment, and using his power to save Mary's life. The psalmist reminds us in 11:7 that, "The Lord is righteous, he loves righteousness, his countenance beholds the upright."

God's word demands that we seek righteousness, that we walk upright and holy in all of our dealings. God loves righteousness because this godly characteristic is the norm for spiritual integrity. For Joseph, this meant turning a difficult situation into one of salvation and blessing.

To live righteously is a call to do the right thing and live the godly way for the right reasons. It means to follow the precepts and principles of God's word in daily living. Righteous means doing the right thing not because you have to, but because you want to. We do right by others in the affairs of life, business, family, church, and community.

Sometimes righteousness can be a costly ordeal. In a world where lying, cheating, stealing, and immorality reign, it is often a challenge to live as godly men and women.

A congregation I served experienced this challenge with a real estate agent. Many in the community knew this agent as a Christian who attended a local church. Through him, we made a deal to purchase some land, but the deal did not go through. The agent received the refund check for tens of thousands of dollars. Rather than returning the money to us immediately, the agent used this money for several months for personal gain and profit. After numerous lies and stalling, the truth finally came out that the agent had misused our funds. Nevertheless, he insisted that he had done nothing wrong. The unrighteousness of the agent only bred more unrighteousness.

This agent was righteous in the negative sense of the word. He called himself a Christian, but his actions were a feigned righteousness. A solemn, sanctimonious righteousness caused his downfall. Rather than living out of a sense of moral excellence, he behaved with a deceptively pious self-assurance.

What can men do to live lives of righteousness? Every day we must examine our activities and actions in light of personal prayer and reflection. We must read the scriptures with an eye toward molding our lives into the image of the Savior. We must be on personal quests to learn the Bible and the precepts of God. We must make every effort to remove habits and relationships that do not draw us closer to God. As we do so, we must cultivate a sense of self-understanding that says we have yet to arrive at the place where God wants us to be. Seeking righteousness is a life-long experience and journey.

REFLECTION JOURNAL

Find a quiet time and place where you will not be disturbed for this experience. Light a candle to remind you of God's presence with you.

Read 2 Samuel 11-12

These two chapters may seem long at first glance. But read them in their entirety in one sitting. Reflect on the characters and try to assign a feelings to the experiences you would have if you were in their shoes. While David made his confession and received forgiveness, there were still consequences for his unrighteousness.

Questions for Reflection

- In what ways did David fail to be righteous?
- What difference has living righteously made in your life?
- What do you need to confess?
- Who suffers when you are unrighteous?
- How have you suffered from unrighteousness?
- What decisions do you need to make today to live a righteous life?

Prayer

Loving God, help me to learn from the past mistakes and failures in my life and relationships. Heal any wounds I may have inflicted because of my unrighteousness and sin. Help me daily to live in peace, patience, and goodness with those around me. Help me to be just and fair in all that I do. Assist me to walk this path I have chosen for my life. Amen.

CHAPTER FIVE

Family

> Now when they had departed, behold,
> an angel of the Lord appeared to Joseph
> in a dream, saying, "Arise, take the
> young child and His mother, flee to
> Egypt, and stay there until I bring you
> word; for Herod will seek the young
> child to destroy Him."
>
> Matthew 2:13 (*NKJV*)

Fidelity: *refers to reliability and devotion
to a duty; faithfulness, loyalty, and truthfulness*

Narrative

Abandonment, neglect, abuse, and violence; the
media is full of stories about men and their disregard for women and children. All too often,
we read about child molestation, abuse, and
neglect at the hands of a father, husband, or
lover. Great numbers of men are in prison

because of a moment of passion or anger that caused them to lay their hands upon a woman or child, causing death or harm. Rather than protecting those who are least able to protect themselves, men are too often the perpetrators of pain and suffering. This is not a pretty picture, and God is not pleased.

This neglect and disregard play themselves out in not only physical forms, but emotional, financial, spiritual, and moral forms as well. The tearing down of the soul of women and children by men is evil. The literature on this subject is sated with reasons and rationale for this epidemic of suffering and sorrow.

Rarely, if ever, do we hear about the countless men who day in and day out care for the women and children in their lives. That kind of news does not sell newspapers or make the television talk shows. Every day in communities everywhere, men are striving to be their best, and God is pleased with them and their behaviors. We constantly tout family values and responsible parenthood, and yet we rarely celebrate them with real and living examples of men doing just that. Our politicians are obsessed with the notion that they can be elected or re-elected if they push the family-values button and stand against anyone and anything that threatens those values. Perhaps we can glean something on this subject from the real-life experiences of Joseph.

What does it mean to protect your family? Certainly, it is not the idea of male, brute-force power. The days of cavemen going out to fight marauding bands of warriors are over. No, the protection we are calling for is different. It means to live a life that keeps and protects your family from life's perils and dangers, seen and unseen. There are financial dangers brought on by unbridled spending and the consumption of goods and services. It means protecting your family from hardship because of premature death due to overeating, smoking cigarettes, poor exercise regimes, and ignoring medical issues. It means conducting yourself in a way that gets you rewarded for your work and vocation and not constantly fired and looking for a job. It means dealing with your personal, psychological, and mental health issues in order to be present and emotionally available to your spouse and children. One of the best ways to protect your family is to be sure that you are doing all that you can to take care of yourself.

I have counseled several couples where one

of them was having or had had an affair with another person outside the marriage. I even counseled a married woman who said she had an "emotional" affair with a man, but they did not have sex. The guilty spouse often did not seem to understand that much of the anger over the affair was because his or her partner felt cheated of the emotional, spiritual, financial, and physical support that was missing from her or his own home. The cheating spouse often never understood that taking those kinds of human affections and resources outside the home had caused some irreparable damage to the marriage. In other words, it was not so much that the partner cheated as much as it was that he or she denied his or her spouse the emotional presence necessary to sustain the relationship. The spouse and children did not feel protected. They all felt cheated and demeaned by the experience.

Let us turn to Joseph and glean lessons from his family experience. Christian love is the kind of love that increases one's desire to grow in grace and spirit. It is the kind of love that wants others to grow in the same ways. Joseph shows us such a love for himself, his wife, and infant child. Again, we have no words from the mouth of Joseph to know what was taking place within him at this point. However, we can see that he put his family first.

Matthew records the dreams and actions of a man committed to God and the protection of his family. Being a man of the Spirit, Joseph paid attention to his dreams and followed the command of the angel to flee the area. He packed up the family, pulled up all stakes, gathered his belongings, and fled. He did not argue about loss of personal property, crops, or other material concerns. Simply put, at the word of God, he did as directed. Why? Joseph chose to protect his family.

This call for men to protect their families does not mean that women are weak and powerless and must turn to men for safety, security, and protection. There is a partnership at work when it comes to raising children, making a safe home, and living in harmony. Nor are we saying families are less valuable when a male figure is absent. We are saying that men must understand their unique roles in relationship to families. Theirs is a special call to cherish women and to protect and nurture children.

Making It Real Every Day

> Each of you, however, should love his wife as himself, and a wife should respect her husband (Ephesians 5:33, *NRSV*).

This is not the time or the place to argue about the difficulties we have with Paul's teachings about men, women, and marriage. However, we need to draw some important details out of these passages in Ephesians and other places. His teachings are important for us to struggle with in terms of how we love and draw close to our families.

Paul speaks first to the wife about her husband. Paul calls upon her to be willing to follow the leadership of the husband. For the husband this means equally to put aside his own needs and desires and put the wife's needs and desires first. Submission is rarely a problem in homes where Christ is the example and the center and where each partner is concerned about the welfare and emotional support of the other partner.

Paul wanted Christians to submit to one another by choice, not law. According to the scripture, the husband is the head of the house, not the dictator. According to scripture, the wife is the spiritual leader of the house, not the doormat. The husband must equally love his wife as the wife seeks to respect the husband. A wise and Christ-honoring husband will be blessed by a wise and Christ-honoring wife. Someone has to balance the checkbook, take out the garbage, change the oil in the car, do laundry, pick up the kids, cut the grass, rake the yard, plan for the kids, take care of relatives.

You might be asking at this point how you are going to make this real in your life. Every couple and partnership does it differently and on its own terms. How can you do this with Christ as the center? Let's begin with men taking responsibility for their end of the relationship. What kind of home life does the Bible call us to create?

- **Create a home that exhibits honor, respect, and communication.** You have to work to establish these characteristics and not to accept things as they are. Relationships are never stable. They are always changing, growing or dying.
- **Have an honest and realistic view of people.** People, including you, are frail, feeble, broken, and sinful.

Accept it! But they are also capable, by God's grace, of forgiveness, compassion, generosity, and love.

- **Have an honest and realistic view of yourself.** Whatever you think of others, good or bad, there you go. What if everybody in the world were just like you? We have to be aware of our projections and personal disorders.
- **Let each other make mistakes.** No one is perfect, especially you. Rarely have I heard anyone take responsibility for troubled or failed relationships. It's always the other person's fault.
- **Deal with problems while they are small, not when they become monsters.** Over time, everything changes, including people and relationships. What was acceptable last week may be a problem this week. Communication is more important now than ever. Few of us communicate well, but never give up on demanding to be heard and listened to and understood. When you quit

demanding to be heard, then you begin to die.

- **Have a willingness to sacrifice anything for the other.** What are you willing to give up for the other? I do not mean just the remote control for the evening. My wife needed to quit her job in order to complete her education. Both of us made sacrifices. However, in order for her to become what God wanted her to become, there needed to be sacrifice. Who knows what the next sacrifice will be?

- **Make the well-being of the other a priority.** Constantly ask, "How will what I do or say affect my wife, partner, or family?" Dying to self and putting others first are spiritual disciplines.

- **Christ is the center and not the culture.** It's not about jobs, new cars, the mall, clothes, cell phones, education, degrees, promotions, and fancy vacations. It's about knowing that the beginning and the end of all things is Christ. That's why partners

who pray together and worship and
praise God together stay together
longer.

- **Each person has to be on a path to
  personal spiritual growth.** You must
  be about the business of growing
  your relationship with God.

These are not simple platitudes that can be
merely applied like a salve. These ideas and
actions call for life-changing discipline and a
spiritual rigor.

REFLECTION JOURNAL

Find a quiet place where you will not be disturbed for this experience. Light a candle to
remind you of God's presence with you.

Read 1 Corinthians 13:1-13

Think about your spouse or family as you read
the passage in its entirety. Then go back and put
the word "our" before you read the word "love"
in every instance. For example, you will say, "our
love is patient and kind" or "our love never ends."
In this way, you personalize Paul's exhortations.
When you have finished, respond to these state-
ments about yourself, your home, and your
relationships with those who live there with
you:

"I can go on in love because . . ."
"In order for me to go on I need to . . ."

Rest in the Word

Sit quietly and feast on the Word and your reflections. Reflect on your responses to this experience. You may want to write down in a journal new insights, revelations, joys, and concerns. Think about ways you can share this experience with those around you.

Prayer

Loving God, as far as it is possible with me, let me be at peace and harmony with those around me. May my life be free from jealousy, boasting, selfish insistence, irritability, rudeness, and selfish ambition. Fill me, loving God, with patience, kindness, gratitude, hope, and joyful expectation. In the name of Jesus I pray. Amen.

Advent-Christmas Gleanings for Men

This study guide consists of five sessions, one hour each. Carefully consider all aspects of this small-group experience before you begin. Do you have the adequate time to see the project through to the end? Have you invited men who will participate fully in the project? Reflect on these and other questions before you begin. There is a Weekly Group Reflection Guide for each of the five chapters of this book.

Many men feel isolated and alone in their spiritual journeys. Christian men everywhere are going it alone, just getting by, or have given up on their spiritual growth. For men to be effective in their walks with God, they need to connect with other believers. A small-group study will allow this connection to happen.

Accountability: Holding Each Other Up in Prayer

This small-group experience encourages men on their journey through mutual support, prayer, and meaningful dialogue. Each participant must agree to be held accountable for his participation in the group through prayer, attendance, and sharing. Each participant must keep in mind:

- Only the Holy Spirit can bring about change in our lives.
- We must always respect one another.
- We are not here to fix one another.
- We must be gentle yet firm with one another out of Christian love.
- We must always answer for ourselves by speaking in the first person.
- We must guard each other's dignity and respect boundaries at all times.
- Confidentiality is a must.

Setting Up the Group

Take the following steps to insure a successful group:

1. Be clear about the purpose of this small group.

   Invite the men to share their reflections and insights about the resources. A successful group consists of four to twelve men. If the group is larger than twelve, form a second group.

2. Decide how you will announce the group.

   Who will lead the group? Will the men take turns, or will there be one leader?

   How will men be invited to attend?

   How will they register their attendance?

3. Decide on the start-up date, time, and location of the group's meetings.

4. When will the group end? A clearly defined meeting schedule is essential.

Weekly Meeting Agenda

- The group gathers—create a welcoming atmosphere. Greet each member, and offer light refreshments, and music.

- The group worships—a time of prayer, singing, and celebration. Services of morning or evening praise and prayer can work well.
- The group shares—a brief time of personal update by each member.
- The groups discusses and reflects—get into the content of the reflection guide for the week, share personal stories, insights, and gleanings from the reading.
- The group gets ready for next time—what leaders and participants need to prepare for the next session.
- The group encourages one another—close the meeting with prayer and words of personal encouragement to one another.

Week One: Commitment

An Experience of Holy Reading

The Parable of the Two Sons (Matthew 20: 28-32)

The point of the Parable of the Two Sons is that doing is more important than saying. James 1:22 exhorts us to "be doers of the word, and not hearers only, deceiving yourselves." Our hearing and doing the word have to do with our commitment.

*The scripture reading for this week is Matthew 20:28-32. We will use a modified process of **lectio divina** or **holy reading**. This is an ancient form of scripture reading that allows the reader to enter into the passage at a much deeper level. We will hear the passage read four times, each time using a different version of the Bible. After each reading, we will reflect on the questions that follow.*

FIRST READING: LET US HEAR THE WORD

Listen to the scripture read by a member of the group. Simply hear what is being read. Do not follow along with your Bible; just hear the words. Listen attentively for a word or phrase from the passage that stands out for you.

Key Question: What do I hear in the passage for me, personally?

The word or phrase might come from the passages itself, and yet it need not be central to the passage. You need not understand why this word or phrase stands out for you. And you do not need to explain or defend your choice to yourself, to the group, or to God. You simply want to consent to receiving the word for yourself and your journey.

After the group hears the passage, enter into a moment or two of silence. Then share with the group that word or phrase without any explanation or comment with the group.

SECOND READING: LET US REFLECT ON THE WORD

Let's read the passage again from a different version of the Bible. As you hear the second reading, listen to the passage and reflect on your life and journey during this Advent and Christmas season.

Key Question: Today, is God pleased with the commitments I have made?

After this second reading, there will be another moment of silence. Then everyone may share his insights.

THIRD READING: LET US RECEIVE GOD'S INVITATION

The passage will be read again from a different version of the Bible. While you are listening to the reading, consider the question, "Do I sense that this passage is inviting me to do or be something in the next few days? Personally, what do I sense this passage is calling me to do or be right now?"

Key Question: What is God inviting me to be, to do?

After a moment of silence, share your reflections with the statement, "I believe God wants me to . . . ."

FINAL READING: LET US PRAY FOR ONE ANOTHER

Join hands in a circle as you listen and hear the scripture passage read one more time. After this, you are invited to pray aloud for the person to your right. In your prayer, lift up the concerns of the person to your right expressed in the Bible study or pray for whatever the Spirit may inspire you to pray for and about. End your prayer with "amen" so the next person will know to begin praying.

Pray for God to help the person on your right respond to the invitation, "What is God inviting me to be, to do." The purpose of the prayer is to affirm God's desire to enable a response to the invitation. Feel free to include a few words of personal thanksgiving for the brother to the right; but at this time, the prayer's focus is on acknowledging that the prayers of those present and God's own call support the individual's desire to be more faithful.

End by embracing one another and offering words of hope and encouragement for the week ahead.

Week Two: Awareness

Below is a narrative, an idea of what Joseph might have been thinking the night his first-born son came into the world. Read the narrative aloud with each member of the group taking a turn. At the end of the reading, pause for a few moments of silence before you begin your sharing.

Joseph and Mary: A Trip to Bethlehem

Bethlehem. I had never been so far from home. It was about an eighty-mile journey. I walked the whole way while Mary rode on a donkey. Some important men in the Roman government had called for a counting of all the people under their control. So we had to make the trip. It was not an option for those of us who were obedient and followed the law. But it could not have come at a worse time in our lives.

It was winter, and Mary was heavy with child. This had been a difficult pregnancy. After all, this was no ordinary baby! The baby was due any day now, not to mention all the stir that had come with the birth announcement. We were betrothed but not yet married. What a mess! But I stuck with her; I stayed by her side. I let go of my rights as a Jewish man, and I ignored the pleas of my friends and admonitions from my family. They all meant well. But they just did not understand. So, I took Mary to be my wife though I was not the father of the child. I stayed by her side. I could do nothing else.

When we arrived in Bethlehem, there were more people in town than I had ever seen or could even imagine. I went from inn to inn looking for a room. Mary must have seen the relief on my face when I came out of the last one. There were no rooms, but the innkeeper gave us permission to sleep and stay in the barn for the night. It was a good thing because

Mary's labor pains were beginning. It was clear that this extraordinary pregnancy and extraordinary child would lead to an extraordinary birth. I stayed by her side. I could do nothing else.

It was a relief to get inside and out of the cold and wind. We were used to sharing space with animals, and we appreciated their warmth and company. They seemed to sense that something special was going on. They became strangely quiet and calm and seemed to know that we were their friends. I found some kindling and build a small fire. It was impossible to make Mary comfortable with the pains growing stronger. I gave her some water and food and did the best I could. Oh, how I wished for the midwife. But there was no going back out to find one. Then Mary's struggle began in earnest, the struggle new life goes through to enter the world. I stayed by her side. I could do nothing else.

The baby struggled to be born, Mary moaned with pain, and I stood ready to receive. And later that night, early the next morning really, Mary delivered our first-born child, a son. I washed him with the water from the trough where the animals drank. Then I wrapped him in the swaddling clothes we had brought from home. The newborn could not sleep on the cold floor with us. I put clean hay in the manger where the animals ate, and there I placed the child.

Then we all tried to get some sleep. You can imagine how startled I was when the barn door creaked opened, and the cold draft blew in. There stood dozens of people: shepherds, villagers, and some children, girls and boys. There were even some Roman soldiers. Suddenly the barn was filled with people and a bright heavenly light. They all seemed to know that we were there and that a baby boy had been born. The women tended to Mary, and the men helped me with the animals and the fire. On a common table we placed our bits of food, wine, and water. Taken together, it seemed like a small feast. Mary smiled and was comforted. I stayed by her side. I could do nothing else.

Then the shepherds shared their amazing story. They had been watching their flocks deep into the night. There had appeared to them angels singing, and there had been a bright and blinding heavenly light. They feared for their lives, and they had heard the angels say, "Fear not."

Their story was even more amazing because the angels had instructed them to go into Bethlehem to find this barn in the back of an inn. The angels had said that they would find a baby wrapped in swaddling clothes, the Savior, Christ the Lord. So they had left their sheep unprotected and walked the five miles into town. It had taken them a while to find us, but someone had told them about a man and a woman riding a donkey who had arrived late and who were staying in the innkeeper's barn near the edge of town.

We wondered what this could mean. We read scripture and talked of good things. We said prayers and thanksgivings to God for the safe birth of the child. We offered blessings for Mary. We thanked God for the angels' visit and pondered what all of this could mean.

Questions for Reflection

1. Mary and Joseph were a young couple in the midst of a life-changing trip to Bethlehem. Have you ever made what you would call an extraordinary journey like Mary and Joseph? Reflect on the details of that journey. How were you

changed and how did God speak to you through that experience?

2. From the narrative, we see Joseph refusing to give up on Mary and their hopes and dreams. Have there been times in your life when you stuck to something even though everyone around you said give it up? Reflect on the details of how you may have stood by someone in their time of need. Reflect on the cost to you personally when you stood by that person and how you were blessed by God.

3. Surely Mary and Joseph's ordeal turned into great joy when the child was born. When have you experienced what Paul calls, "joy unspeakable?" In other words, reflect on those times when joy was great and powerful in your life.

Close with prayer for your family and friends. Ask God to show you how to be a committed man in their lives.

Week Three: Discipline

An Experience of Holy Reading

To Be Disciplined Means To Make Sacrifices (Romans 12:1-8)

In Romans 12:1-8, Paul calls us to a new discipline: to be different in this world because we have Christ in our lives. Paul calls us to be disciplined in the transformation and renewal of our minds, our bodies, our gifts, and our spirits.

*The scripture reading for this week is Romans 12:1-8. We will use a modified process of **lectio divina** or **holy reading**. See week one for instructions regarding this practice.*

Week Four: Righteousness

An Experience of Holy Reading

Walking in Righteousness: Living As Men of Light (Ephesians 4:17-32)

In Ephesians 4:17-32, Paul admonishes us to walk in righteousness. "Walk" refers to our daily conduct as believers. In these verses, Paul first talks about the conduct of unbelievers. In 4:20-24, Paul talks about shedding the old self and putting on the new

*because we are now in Christ. In 4:25-32, Paul
outlines how we will be transformed and changed
when we walk in the Lord in righteousness.*

*The scripture reading for this week is
Ephesians 4:17-32. We will use a modified process
of **lectio divina** or **holy reading**. See week one for
instructions regarding this practice.*

Week Five: Family

An Experience of Holy Reading

Husbands and Wives: Walking Together in Wisdom (Ephesians 5:15-33)

*Paul exhorts us in Ephesians to walk together in
wisdom with our mates, respecting and submitting
to one another out of love. Every spirit-filled
Christian is to be a humble and submissive
Christian. This is foundational to all relationships.
The basis for intimacy, love, and beauty in our
relationships grows out of our reverence for God,
our creator.*

*The scripture reading for this week is
Ephesians 5:15-33. We will use a modified process
of **lectio divina** or **holy reading**. See week one for
instructions regarding this practice.*